Life Cycle of a
Pumpkin

Ron Fridell
and
Patricia Walsh

Heinemann Library
Chicago, Illinois

Designed by Wilkinson Design
Illustrated by David Westerfield
Printed and bound in China by South China Printing Company.

06 05
10 9 8 7 6 5 4

Library of Congress Cataloging-in-Publication Data
Fridell, Ron.
    Life cycle of a pumpkin / Ron Fridell, Patricia Walsh.
        p. cm.
Includes bibliographical references (p.) and index.
    ISBN 1-58810-093-6
    1. Pumpkin—Life cycles—Juvenile literature. [1. Pumpkin.] I. Title:
Pumpkin. II. Walsh., Patricia, 1951- III. Title.
    SB347 .F75 2001
        635'.62—dc21
                        00-011234

Acknowledgments
The Publisher would like to thank the following for permission to reproduce photographs:
Ben Klaffe, pp. 4, 13, 16, 17, 29; Corbis/Phil Schermeister, p. 5; Photodisc/Santokh Kochar, pp.
6, 28; Dwight Kuhn, pp. 7, 8, 9, 11, 14, 15, 19, 20, 25, 28, 29; Index Stock/Shmuel Taylor, p. 10;
Index Stock/Steve Solum, pp. 12, 28; Corbis/Reuters New Media Inc., p. 18; Corbis/Philip Gould,
p. 21; Corbis/Barry Lewis, p. 22; Corbis/Matthew Klein, p. 23; PictureQuest/PhotoEdit/Tony
Freeman, p. 24; Corbis/Richard T. Nowitz, p. 26; Corbis/Richard Hamilton Smith, p. 27;
Corbis/Mark Gibson, p. 29.

Cover photograph: Dwight Kuhn

Some words are shown in bold, **like this.** You can
·find out what they mean by looking in the glossary.

Contents

What Is a Pumpkin?

A pumpkin is a fruit. It grows on a
vine like other kinds of **squash.**
Pumpkins can be bumpy or smooth,
large or small, long or round. They
can be orange, white, yellow, or red.

Seed

1 week

2 weeks

10 weeks

Each year there is a new **crop** of pumpkins.
Their hard shells have deep lines that go
from top to bottom.

11 weeks

14 weeks

16 weeks

Seed

Spring

6

Pumpkins begin as **seeds.** The seeds are white and have an oval shape. A tiny plant is curled up inside each seed.

Seed

1 week

2 weeks

10 weeks

The seed is planted in warm, moist soil. In about ten days, a root grows down into the soil. The root takes in water and food for the plant. Tiny leaves push up into the sunlight.

11 weeks

14 weeks

16 weeks

Seedling

The first two leaves pop through the soil. These are smooth **seed** leaves. They use sunlight and air to make food for the new plant.

8

Seed

I week

2 weeks

10 weeks

Then the true leaves appear. They are
jagged and prickly. The job of the seed
leaves is done. They **wither** and fall off.

Vine Early summer

The pumpkin plant grows more leaves. The plant grows quickly and soon becomes a **vine.** The vine twists and creeps along the ground.

Seed

1 week

2 weeks

10 weeks

The vine sends out thin **tendrils.** They grab and curl around other vines. They twist around fences. The tendrils support the vine as it grows longer and longer.

11 weeks

14 weeks

16 weeks

Flower   Early summer

The pumpkin **vine blooms** with
many yellow flowers. Some of these
are female flowers. Female flowers
sit on small, fuzzy green balls.

Seed   1 week   2 weeks   10 weeks

Other flowers are male flowers. They are on long stems and have yellow powder inside the flower. The yellow powder is **pollen.** It takes a male and a female flower to make a pumpkin.

11 weeks   14 weeks   16 weeks

Pollination

It also takes bees to make pumpkins. They move the **pollen** from male flowers to female flowers. When a bee visits the male flowers, the pollen sticks to the bee's body and legs.

14

Seed

1 week

2 weeks

10 weeks

The pollen rubs off the bee as it goes in and out of the flowers. When the pollen reaches a female flower, the fuzzy green ball at the end of the flower begins to grow into a pumpkin.

11 weeks   14 weeks   16 weeks

Growing and Ripening

Late summer

All summer the **vines, tendrils,** and leaves of the plant grow and tangle together. Underneath the big leaves are little pumpkins.

Seed

1 week

2 weeks

10 weeks

The leaves are like big umbrellas. They keep the hot sun off the pumpkins. They also help to keep the soil around the pumpkins from drying out.

11 weeks

14 weeks

16 weeks

Problems for Pumpkins

Growing pumpkins need just the
right amount of water and sun.
Too much rain **rots** the pumpkins.
Too much sun **withers** the **vines.**

Seed

1 week

2 weeks

10 weeks

Cucumber beetles and **squash** bugs can hurt pumpkins, too. Farmers spray the plants with **insecticides** or cover the vines with nets to protect the growing pumpkins.

11 weeks

14 weeks

16 weeks

Harvest

The pumpkins grow bigger and bigger. Inside, the pumpkins form **seeds** and **pulp.** Outside, the pumpkins turn from green to orange.

Seed

1 week

2 weeks

10 weeks

Then the **vines** turn brown. **Harvest**
time has come. The farmer cuts the
thick pumpkin stem from the vine.

11 weeks

14 weeks

16 weeks

After the Harvest Late fall

Four months ago there were only **seeds.** Now the farmer has **harvested** a wagon full of round, orange pumpkins. They will be sold at farmstands and stores.

Seed

1 week

2 weeks

10 weeks

People cook pumpkins and use the **pulp** to make pumpkin pie, cookies, soup, and bread. Some pumpkins are fed to farm animals.

11 weeks

14 weeks

16 weeks

Some towns hold a pumpkin **festival** to celebrate the fall **harvest.** Sometimes there is a contest to find out who grew the biggest pumpkin.

Seed

1 week

2 weeks

10 weeks

Many pumpkins are scooped out and carved to make jack-o'-lanterns. People put candles inside jack-o'-lanterns to make them glow with a warm, orange light.

11 weeks

14 weeks

16 weeks

Inside the pumpkin are many **seeds.**
Some seeds are roasted to be eaten
as a snack. Other seeds are saved to
be planted in the spring. They will
grow into next year's pumpkins.

Seed

1 week

2 weeks

10 weeks

After the pumpkins are picked and sold, the farmer **plows** the field. Old **vines** and unpicked pumpkins get mixed with the soil. The field is ready for planting seeds again next spring.

11 weeks

14 weeks

16 weeks

Life Cycle

1 Seed

2 Seedling

3 Vine and Flowers

4 Pollination

5 Growing Pumpkin

6 Harvest

29

Fact File

The biggest pumpkin on record was grown in Ontario, Canada, in 1998. It weighed as much as a large horse!

Native Americans dried strips of pumpkin and wove them into mats.

Different kinds of pumpkins have different names, such as Sugar Pie, Atlantic Giant, Baby Boo, and Cinderella.

Connecticut Field Pumpkins usually weigh as much as two or more large bags of sugar.

A pumpkin **vine** might have flowers all summer, but each flower **blooms** for only one day.

Glossary

bloom to have flowers

crop food grown in one season

festival special time of celebration

harvest gathering of a crop

insecticide poison that kills insects

plow to turn over and mix up the soil

pollen grains of yellow powder that are released from male flowers

pulp soft, fleshy part of a fruit or vegetable

rot decay; spoil

seed part of a plant that can grow into a new plant

squash fruit like a pumpkin

tendril long, thin part of a plant stem that grabs and curls around things to help the plant climb or spread

vine plant with long, thin stems that grow along the ground or climb up things

wither dry up; shrivel

More Books to Read

Gibbons, Gail. *The Pumpkin Book*. New York: Holiday House, 1999.

Hutchings, Amy. *Picking Apples and Pumpkins*. New York: Scholastic, 1994.

Saunders-Smith, Gail. *From Blossom to Fruit*. Mankato, Minn.: Capstone, 1998.

Index